The Story of Moses and God's Promise

by Martina Smith

illustrated by Peter Grosshauser
and Ed Temple

SPARK
HOUSE
FAMILY

MINNEAPOLIS

Pharaoh, the king of Egypt, was afraid. He was rich and powerful, but Pharaoh was scared of God's people, the Hebrews. He was afraid they would try to become more powerful than he was.

2

So Pharaoh made them his slaves and ordered them to work very hard. Worst of all, he demanded that all Hebrew baby boys be drowned in the Nile River.

God's people endured many long, hard years under Pharaoh's rule.

3

During this fearful time, a baby boy was born to a Hebrew mother. She loved him and wanted him to live. So she made a floating basket, put him in it, and then hid it at the edge of the Nile River. The baby's big sister, Miriam, hid near the shore and watched.

Just then, Pharaoh's daughter came down to the river and noticed the basket. When she looked inside, she was surprised to see a baby boy crying.

5

"This must be one of the Hebrews' children," said Pharaoh's daughter. "He's awfully cute! I think I'll keep him and name him Moses."

Miriam bravely stepped out of her hiding place. "I could find someone to help take care of the baby for you," she said.

"That would be perfect!" said Pharaoh's daughter. Miriam told her mother, who took good care of Moses.

When Moses was old enough, he went to live with Pharaoh's daughter. Moses grew up in Pharaoh's palace. During that time, life became worse and worse for God's people.

Years later, Moses was watching his sheep when he saw a strange sight. Flames of fire came from a bush, but the bush did not burn up.

"Moses! Moses!" said a loud voice.

Moses was scared. "Here I am," he said.

"Take off your shoes," the voice thundered. "You are standing on holy ground."

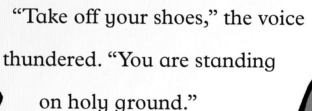

Moses kicked off his sandals. "I am the God of
your fathers," the voice said. Moses was afraid.
"I have heard my people crying," God said,
"and have come to save them. I will give them a
new, safe place to live."

9

Moses thought, "How will God do this?"

God said, "I am sending you to Pharaoh to ask him to let my people go."

"Me?" said Moses. "Who am I to go to Pharaoh? Who am I to lead your people?" He threw himself down onto the ground before God.

But Moses kept one eye on the burning bush.

"I will be with you," God said.

Moses trusted God. He was willing to do everything God said.

Moses became the leader of the Hebrew people. His brother, Aaron, helped lead too. Many Hebrews were forced to be slaves in Egypt. Moses and Aaron went to Pharaoh. They said, "Our God says, 'Let my people go!'"

"I don't believe in your God," shouted Pharaoh. "Now get back to work!"

Ten times, Moses said to Pharaoh, "Let my people go!"

Each time, Pharaoh said, "No!"

So God sent ten plagues to change Pharaoh's mind. First, God turned the Nile River into blood. The people could not drink. And still Pharaoh said, "No!"

Seven days later, God sent frogs. Frogs covered the land and rivers. And still Pharaoh said, "No! I will not let your people go!"

Then God sent swarms of gnats, then flies. Then God struck down all of Pharaoh's herds. A plague of sores was next. Still Pharaoh said, "No!"

In the next plague, God sent a great storm. Hail pounded and thunder crashed. The Egyptians' plants and trees were destroyed. Still Pharaoh said, "No!"

Next, God sent a plague of locusts. The little bugs covered the land. Then came a plague of three days of darkness.

Then God sent the last and saddest plague of all. Every one of the Egyptians' firstborn children died. A loud cry arose from Egypt as the people mourned their loss. Finally, Pharaoh told Moses he would let God's people go.

Leaving Egypt meant a long journey. The Hebrew people camped on the shore of the Red Sea. They were feeling nervous. Would Pharaoh keep his promise?

Soon a cloud of dust rose up in the distance. A rumble of horse hooves thundered toward the travelers. Hundreds of Pharaoh's chariots charged toward them. The soldiers had orders to bring the people back to Egypt.

"We're trapped!" someone yelled. Cries went up from the people. "Moses," they shouted, "have you brought us here to die?!"

19

"Don't be afraid," Moses told the people. "God is with us."

Moses gripped his staff. He shouted into the wind, "We will go through the Red Sea!"

Standing on the edge of the shore, Moses raised his staff over the white waves. The waters trembled and divided.

The wild wind roared. Soon a wall of water stood on the left and the right. Dry land appeared between the walls. A safe path to the other side! "Move now!" Moses ordered. How strange it must have felt to step onto the sandy path. Would God save them? Would God keep the promise to Moses?

In the morning, Pharaoh's army stood on the Red Sea's shore. They saw the people safe on the other side. Pharaoh's army moved slowly across the rocky and sandy path. "They will catch us!" a young woman yelled.

"Watch and wait," said Moses.

Once again, Moses held his staff up over the walls of waves. Tons of water came tumbling down! Horses, chariots, and riders were all swept into the sea.

From the safe shore came the sounds of singing and dancing, led by Miriam, Moses' sister. "Sing to the Lord," the people shouted. "God has saved us!"

Traveling was hard and tiring. The Hebrew people had never lived outside of Egypt. They were afraid, but God went with them as they walked long and far to the place God promised.

Along the way, the people became hungry. They complained to Moses. God heard their cries. The next morning, the ground was covered with tiny pieces of bread called manna. God had sent manna for the people to eat.

Later, the people ran out of water. God told Moses to hit a rock with his staff. When he did, water gushed out of the rock. God took care of the people, just like God promised.

With God watching over them, the people walked and walked and walked over the hot, dry land.

One morning, something incredible happened. A dark cloud covered Mount Sinai. Lightning and thunder filled the sky. The people were afraid.

Suddenly, the voice of God called Moses.

God told Moses to climb to the top of the mountain. When he got to the top, God spoke. God gave Moses important rules for the people to live by. Moses told them, "These rules will help you love God and each other."

When the Hebrew people were close to the place God had promised, Moses said, "Come here. I have a message from God!" Everyone turned to listen. "There is only one God," said Moses, "and we are part of God's family! Love God with everything you say, think, and do!"

The people were thankful for the new country God was giving them. They knew it was important to remember God in their new home. Moses said, "Teach your children about God."

The people did remember God. They told their children stories about God. They were God's family.

Making Faith Connections: A Note to Adults

Sharing a Bible story with a child can be a wonderful time to grow your faith together. Here are a few suggestions for ways you can enrich a child's engagement and learning with this book.

 Did you notice Squiggles, the expressive caterpillar who appears throughout the book? When you see Squiggles, ask your child how Squiggles is feeling. Then ask why Squiggles feels that way. Invite the child to share about a time they felt the same way Squiggles does.

 Discuss with your child how it was hard for Moses to do what God asked. Ask them to tell you about something hard they have had to do.

 Talk with your child about the ten plagues that God brought to Egypt. Ask him or her to think of what it would be like to see that many frogs. What if there were flies or gnats buzzing everywhere?

 God provided food and water for the Israelites during their journey. Ask your child what God has provided for them and for their family.

Bible Connections

This picture book is based on the following Bible texts: Exodus 2:1-10; 3:1-15; 5:1—6:13; 7:14—12:32; 14:1-30; 16:1-18; 17:1-7; 20:1-17.

The Ten Commandments

Talk with your child about how your family works together to follow the Ten Commandments. For example, how do we honor God? How does our family rest on the Sabbath?

I am God, the only God. Honor me above all other things and people.

There are no other gods for you, only me.

My name is special. Don't use it with bad words or mean talk.

Take a day of rest each week. Call it the Sabbath, and make it a special day for God.

Show your mom, dad, and others who take care of you love and respect.

Don't hurt others with your words or actions.

If you get married, you must be loyal to your husband or wife.

Don't take things that aren't yours.

Tell only the truth about your family, friends, and even those you do not know.

Be happy with what you have. Don't wish for things that other people have.

24 23 22 21 20 19 18 17 16 15   1 2 3 4 5 6 7 8

Hardcover ISBN: 978-1-4514-9982-7

E-book ISBN: 978-1-4514-9983-4

Cover design: Alisha Lofgren
Book design: Eileen Z. Engebretson

Library of Congress Cataloging-in-Publication Data

Smith, Martina, author.
  The story of Moses and God's promise : a spark Bible story / by Martina Smith ; illustrated by Peter Grosshauser and Ed Temple.
      pages cm. — (Spark bible stories)
  Audience: Ages 3–7.
  Audience: K to grade 3.
  ISBN 978-1-4514-9982-7 (alk. paper)
1. Moses (Biblical leader)—Juvenile literature. 2. Exodus, The—Juvenile literature. 3. Bible stories, English—Exodus. I. Grosshauser, Peter, illustrator. II. Temple, Ed, illustrator. III. Title.
  BS580.M6S53 2015
  222.109209505—dc23
                        2015010812

Printed on acid-free paper.

Printed in U.S.A.

V63474; 9781451499827; AUG2015